Within and around us, we wrestle with angels and demons, both shaping and frustrating our journey. Our souls cry out to the Lord in the struggle, often leaving us limping, our hips put out of joint, yet it is in this sacred wrestling that we are named and known. In life, there is no predetermined victory—only the unfolding reality of our pilgrim walk. The path is marked by the places where we stopped to grapple, the moments of struggle that reveal who we are becoming. It is in these encounters, with the divine and the broken alike, that our identity takes shape. Let us pray.

C. Andrew Doyle

Wrestling with Angels and Demons:

Prayers At Faith's Edge

By C. Andrew Doyle

Table of Contents

A Fore-Warning

I have had a good life, for which I am grateful. I have also lived through tough times. I have experienced hard spiritual trials. I have prayed, sometimes filled with assurance and sometimes filled with doubt. I have prayed the prayer of the sinner because that is what I am. I have wrestled with demons—both my own and others'. I have wrestled with angels. I have heard the shuffle of angels' wings and walked with the black dog and its demons at my heels. I have discovered that the grace of God is a two-edged sword: the assurance of heavenly goodness and the knowledge that I live by grace alone. These cut both ways and bring me to my knees if I stop and think about it. God cuts me down, just as Odetta Holmes sang (Odetta Holmes, "God's Gonna Cut You Down," 1956). God cuts me down both ways.

I've lived long enough to be content, having seen enough. I get up in the morning and give thanks for rising another day. I go to bed and give thanks for having lived another day. I give thanks for my life, which is genuinely filled with love, family, and friends. Yet I know that brokenness surrounds me, but I trust and hope. Sometimes I search for the smallest amount of grace because, on those days, I feel broken myself. There can be a lot of those days in a row. So, truth be told, many of my prayers are offered at the edge of faith.

Maybe this is the cost of being a pastor. I know I need Jesus.

I love a song or two about sin and redemption. I've got a lot of them on a playlist called "The Devil, God, and Me." The next one is from *The Grifter's Hymnal* by Ray Wylie Hubbard. He has influenced me a lot over the years. It goes like this:

When darkness swoops down on you,

Ask God for some light.

When some devil knocks you down,

Ask God to pick you up.

When death comes a-knocking,

Ask God to open the door.

(Hubbard, "Ask God," 2012, used here by permission.)

This is a forewarning. These are my prayers; some I have shared, some I have not. You might say, "That pastor shouldn't pray that way." But I do. I do pray this way. So take warning, my friend.

In this book, I hope you can find some solace when you are out of words or need some. Maybe you pray without opening the book, holding it for comfort. Perhaps you pray through it like one of my grandmother's hand-worn books, and over time, you add your own prayers and notes to it. I don't know how you will use it, but I imagine the best way will be your way.

I am letting you in on a little secret. These are the prayers of the sin-sick soul. By praying these words, I learn I can jump up because of Jesus' grace! As Ray Wylie Hubbard promises: whoopin' and hollerin'. For Jesus has promised that I have been set free and no longer need to be burdened by my sin. I have been forgiven. I can only get there through honest, sin-soaked prayers. But I know, like many others before me, that my Redeemer lives and goes now to prepare a place for me. "So, when I rise up in God's empyrean heaven, I'll be flappin' my angel wings, and on that day, I'm gonna whoop, I'm gonna holler" (Hubbard, *A. Enlightenment, B. Endarkenment*, 2010).

When I wrestle with angels and demons at the edge of faith, I remember St. Paul's words from Romans 8:38-39: neither death, nor life, nor angels, nor rulers, nor things present, nor things to come, nor powers, nor height, nor depth, nor anything else in all creation will be able to separate [me] from the love of God in Christ Jesus our Lord.

Introduction

While we struggle—sometimes with our doubts and fears, sometimes with surprise storms that threaten our peace or shatter us to the core—we wrestle together. We never walk alone.

Lifting heavy loads or light gratitude, we gingerly make our way with feeble words and open hearts into the beauty of God's silence. With invisible angels and demons, we wrestle in the dark with fears, doubts, and hopeful dreams. Sometimes, we aren't even sure what troubles rumble inside the breastplates of our hearts, let alone with whom we are wrestling.

The true and honest prayers of the heart are those in which we wrestle with demons and angels and somehow meet God in the midst. Wrestling prayers speak the language of human struggle. I offer you this: a gathering of prayers and thoughts lifted to God from light and darkness.

Most of what follows are prayer poems, like the biblical story of Jacob wrestling with God's angel or Moses's encounter with God in the burning bush, struggling, no doubt, with the fearful joy of hearing God's calling out from the midst of the bush. Several of the prayers are responses from the poet's heart to the losses and sufferings of others. Overall, most of the prayers in this book are 'down-to-earth', which is another way of saying that they speak from the heart of the here and now, from the point of view of a wandering sinner and saint, a fighting prophet, a psalmist crying out in the wilderness, "Where is your comfort, Lord?"

Wrestling is a biblical metaphor that encapsulates the human spirit's gritty, authentic, up-close-and-personal struggle. It tells the story of Jacob, who, in the darkness of night, wrestled with an angel till dawn and wouldn't let go until he received a blessing. That wrestling with God put his hip out of joint—it changed how he could walk his path. The following day, he walked and reconciled with his brother (Genesis 32, 33). It is a poignant reminder that we don't just wrestle with the hardships of life, the irony of the human condition, the loneliness of disconnection from the world, and the demons; we are wrestling with ourselves, the unknown, God, and the angels.

Perhaps it's in our darkest times that we find ourselves on our knees—or want to be on our knees—crying out for help. Then, prayer, long an option, becomes a necessity. It becomes a lifeline. We are drawn to it not because, like the answer, it is within our reach. We are drawn to it because, like the answer, it is desperately needed. We need God's help in the darkest times. We need God's comfort, God's counsel, God's serenity. And sometimes, we need God's word that we are never alone. that the God who made us and the God we may have turned away from still hears us, even when we feel alone in the darkness. It is the idea that we can let go of our struggles and sins, lifting them into God's great bosom—God's memory—and thus be freed and comforted.

But even in our personal prayers, we are asked to reach out to others. It's tempting to get caught in the tragedy of our own suffering. At times, it can feel as though our darkness is the darkest of all. Prayer reminds us that our capacity to pray is an invitation to move beyond the boundaries of who we are and what we are experiencing, to remember those who are also suffering and in need. We pray for them as well as for ourselves. We pray for the worker who labors long night hours, unnoticed. For the child who is alone, afraid, and on the verge of despair. For the stranger who carries burdens too great to bear in isolation. As we do so, we remember that we are part of an interconnected human family, and it is our prayers that reach out to lift others up, even when we have little left to give.

There's another thing we desperately need—thanksgiving. In the wrestling match of our lives, we need to learn to give thanks. We need to find something for which to be grateful, even when it's hard to see. Gratitude helps us see that God is with us, even in the valley of shadows. Thanks is not just for the good times; thanksgiving is a practice for the hard times, too, for the times when we don't know what to do next. It reminds us that there is still loveliness in the world, still light when the path seems dim. Gratitude holds us to God and to each other as we open our hearts to the ever-present divine, the elemental presence that fills all of life.

This book is divided into categories of prayers, each meant to benefit your soul in different ways. But before we get there, let us examine the most fundamental question: what is prayer?

What is Prayer?

At its core, prayer is a response to God—an outward reaching, an urge to enter into dialogue where 'I' and 'Thou' meet, where words give way to silence, and action is as much a part of receptivity as receptivity is a part of action. Through deeds and silence, through the spoken word, prayer is both active and passive, reaching out as well as receiving. At prayer's heart is the lament: I would, I must, I need to connect. The soul's cry reveals the human need for communion. But it is also the prayer of the one who *does not believe* yet dares to hope—a plea of the lost, the sinner, who calls out in anguish, longing, hoping not to go unheard, unfound, unanswered, or unexpectedly beloved.

Prayer is both a pilgrimage—we go seeking God—and a rediscovery that He was never absent. It is a place to which we are called to return, often before we realize that we have already arrived. In prayer, we find that God has been waiting for us all along, that he is found in our desperate pleas, in our tears, confusion, and celebrations.

Another distinguishing feature of Christian prayer is that, as an address to God the Father, it is always directed through the one Mediator—Jesus Christ—in the power of the Holy Spirit. This relationship is distinctively Christian.

Through Christ, we have access to the Father, and through the Holy Spirit, we are empowered to pray with boldness, knowing that our words are heard, our sighs known, and our souls attended to. Christian prayer expresses the poverty of our creatureliness and the abundance of our invitation into divine intimacy.

What Prayer Did Christ Teach Us?

Our Lord gave us a pattern for prayer in the Lord's Prayer. Here, we have a model for how to address God, expressing reverence, humility, and submission to His will—adoration, confession, thanksgiving, and supplication. This is the form of our prayers: seek God's kingdom, trust in His provision, forgive as we have been forgiven, and rely on God for guidance and protection. Here are a few types of Christian prayer you can find in this book.

Adoration: We praise God for who He is – for His greatness, holiness, and love. We think about these things and not our immediate concerns, and we abide in the presence of the Almighty.

Praise: Praise is a reaction of joy and appreciation at what God has done; it celebrates His works, His faithfulness, and His mercy. It remembers His goodness and helps us to trust His purposes.

Thanksgiving: Thanksgiving is a prayer of gratitude, as in the Episcopal Book of Common Prayer: 'It is right to give thanks and praise.' It centers our attention on the many blessings we have and away from the things we lack. It is inherently reorienting, turning a grateful heart towards God and engendering in us the joy of having instead of needing — the joy of contentment.

Penitence: We confess to God our sins and pray to be forgiven. In penitence, we face up to our errors, our mistakes, and our general inadequacy, at the same time as we long to be at one with God again.

Oblation: The offering of ourselves to God – our lives, our work, our struggles, our hopes. It's a prayer: 'Here I am, Lord, use me as You will.'

Intercession: Intercession is prayer on behalf of others. It is a loving act, lifting the world to God, and trusting that He hears and is moved with mercy.

Petition: Petition is the prayer of request – coming to God as one who is in need of his help and care. It is a recognition of our dependence upon him and trust in his provision. There are prayers here in each of these categories and more, a wide range of expressions in approaching God, of finding ourselves in his presence, even arguing with our angel, coming to Him in need.

Whether you need words for joy or sorrow, to repent and forgive, to pay homage or be aware, or to invite God to accompany you along your spiritual path — and to know God's enduring love for you, I hope this book might accompany you along the way. May these prayers remind you that, in wrestling, we are never alone and that God is always with us – in the dark of night, in pain and worry, in the quiet of peace, and in the long nights of struggle.

~ C. Andrew Doyle

A Beginning

1.
Eyes look out defiantly,
breath bespeaks no word,
anger at the fates
or absent God,
whatever faith chosen.
There is no cheating
the dark night of the soul.
Yet God waits patiently,
never bidden,
ever present,
breathing a word of love,
the shadow of
his cross in-breaking the void.
One might ask:
how do I begin?
What to say?
I say begin in quiet.
Then say what you must say.
Ask what you must ask.
Shake your fist,
cry out your pain,
curse,
want,
and hope.
Then let
the quiet
give
a peace beyond you
mercy and grace await.
This is how talking with God begins. Amen.

Prayers I Pray

2.
I have dug
a cluntch pit
in my soul.
By hand,
I have dug it
out to build a life,
despite its porosity
and susceptibility
to weathering.
Take that hole,
garden God,
and ring it
with trees,
grassland flora,
and green habitat.
Help me again
find tranquility
and beauty,
despite the chalk
remaining beneath
my nails. Amen.

("Cluntch" is a chalk building material mined from a pit.)

3.
Our hearts
are restless
until they
rest in thee
I am told;
so mine cries out
for something,
oh how I let it cry
seeking after all
the wrong
solutions.
It cries
for it is crying
for its God
for its father
and mother
and home.
This is why
At times
My world
looks dull and gray,
till my heart is satisfied
and quieted
with the presence of thee. Amen

4.
Help me be silent
for love,
to speak
for love,
to correct and forgive
for love.
Christ,
be the root of
love within me.
Help me to remember love
in adversity
and to love generously
in hospitality.
Help me encounter
love in sacred books,
its virtue in prophecy,
and to see that
it is the richness
of loving
that I discover you. Amen.

5.
God,
I want to hear your voice.
We search
for God online,
in private religion,
in austerity,
in retreat,
and alone,
privatizing
our spiritual pilgrimage.
All the while,
God is present
in the face of friends,
family,
and strangers
worst of all in our enemy's face.
This last is the truth
we cannot stand.
So, our search continues
while God whispers,
"I am here." Amen.

6.
God of love
teach me to love,
I want to
feel the pain of loving.
I want
my eyes opened.
I want to be
Interrupted by
Your love.
I want to live
A love that aches. Amen.

7.
Jesus let your
Love turn
others
against me,
I want to
Be wrestled
to the ground
by this love.
Loose
this love
upon me
cost what it will
lead where it may. Amen

8.
Jesus.
From you,
I get
Mercy
Forgiveness
And grace.
But
Weep
for Your sinner friend,
because I lose my way
and you will weep
as I walk away,
for that's what
You get for lovin' me,
I am grateful
That you wait
For me to wander
Back to you
And stumble
Up the road.
That's what
You get for lovin' me.
And, from you
I get
Mercy
Forgiveness
And grace. Amen.

9.
Shepherding God,
lead me through the desert,
show me straight paths,
 lower the mountains
before me,
reveal the living water,
seek me when lost,
call my name,
and swing wide
the gate so,
by the grace of Your cross,
my sins
may be braced upon it,
that I may enter
Your kingdom. Amen.

10.
O Firstborn,
reveal
how the long
silence
once held
us in its power,
saying: "You are mine,
O child!
I, the silence of death,
am your destiny."
Let us rejoice together,
You and I,
as silence turned
away when it beheld
the mystery of the Lord,
who made the heavens and earth,
who in the beginning made us. Amen.

11.
Come,
risen Lord,
behind my locked
door heart,
where fear lurks,
and shadows
of doubt dance.
Show me
my wounds
reflected in Yours;
invite me to believe.
Then unfix
my feet of clay,
breathe me
out onto
a pilgrim way of love. Amen.

12.
Raise
Raise
my Lazarus bones
and wrapped arms
and legs.
Raise my Lazarus
hands and eyes.
Raise my Lazarus
heart so that,
coming out
of my sleeping tomb,
I may awake
to hear a voice
call me
from my spiced death
into a life of light.
And I might burn
such that
others may discover
a life beyond
the walking dead. Amen.

13.
Dear crucified Lord,
descend into my
protected heart
where
it is haunted
by demons.
Free my sin-sick
soul
that I may join
You in heaven
and follow
Your ways on earth.
You promised
heaven to the thief
because he knew his wrong.
Grant me,
on my day,
such courageous
faith
to ask
entrance into
Your kingdom
and a place
for crumbs
at Your table. Amen.

14.
Dear Lord,
You know
I'm not a perfect man.
I'm not even
a good man,
yet through Christ,
You have made
it so
I'm not
the sum
of my mistakes
or the sum
of all the
good things
I've done.
The truth
lies in
You
and not
between the two.
Lord,
I am a man
who has been loved
well both
by God
and by my family.
I'm a grateful man.
That is good.
So watch over us,
family and friends.
May we walk slow,
go easy,
and love well
till we raise
the parting glass. Amen.

(Inspired by the folk song *The Parting Glass*)

15.
Midnight tolls the bell,
the Banshee cries
shrill my name.
Lord, my heart
too easily reaches
for faulty assurance,
as it quakes
at the sound of
death's final whisper.
So bind my soul
with love that
though
the screech comes ever nigh,
across hill and bog,
I may have the peace
of rest in you. Amen.

(Inspired by the poetry of Francis Duggan)

16.
God of wisdom,
certainty does
not make me free.
Help my faith
be acted upon,
help me love
and truthfully live
so that I
might claim
my freedom
given freely to me. Amen.

17.
Good Lord,
providence leads
to gratitude
in its sense of grace.
For I grow
Little that
I eat,
I make
Nothing
That I wear,
I speak a living
Word
I did
not invent
or speak first.
l am protected
by freedoms
and laws
I did not create
Fight for.
I am moved
by hymns and song
I did not imagine
nor the hardware
and software
that I create with.
So,
I give thanks
to you
great God
for my humanity
among humans
and the cosmos
that affords a
richness of diverse life
to appreciate.
I give great thanks
For the gift to love

and admire
my fellow humanity,
living and dead,
know
I am drawn
ever closer to you.

(Inspired by Steve Job's email to himself, 9.10.2010.)

18.
Death
is the gate
to eternal life.
I have seen a lot
Of death:
young,
old,
rich,
poor,
sudden,
long-suffering,
in sleep,
and in violence.
In all deaths
burdens,
regrets,
and family wounds mar
the only thing
that has mattered all along:
how much you
have loved
and been loved. All else is lost.
Help me be found. Amen.

19.
Show me the mystic,
Lord:
an addict praying,
a doctor before surgery,
an aunt reciting
the Lord's Prayer
over a sister's child
who is not home,
a grandfather
reading a Bible at 5 a.m.,
or a school teacher
whispering students' names
before sleep.
The mystics call on you—teach me. Amen.

20.
The dark hours
are upon me this night;
surround me with your wings,
O Trinity.
Help me mend the ill
I have done.
Humble my pride.
Forgive my misspeech.
All that I might sleep peaceably,
forgiven,
and refreshed
to awake
and do your will.
Tonight,
surround me with your wings, O Trinity. Amen.

21.
Good Lord,
you have given me such
freedom to love you.
Help me to use
this freedom
to love others
with generosity.
Give me also
the freedom
to release control
of those things
that are not mine to control.
Teach me the wisdom of love. Amen

22.
When the moon is low,
the sea is sleeping,
and the song
of the whale
is sung in the deep
God, whisper
to me
of the beauty
that existed
before the world
was known,
and of a love
which weaves
life together. Amen.

23.
May God the Father bless me,
may Christ take care of me,
may the Holy Spirit give light to me,
for I am lost
and I am fumbling towards you.
Lord, be my defender
and keeper of my body
and my soul,
to the ages of ages. Amen.

(Inspired by Æthelwold of Winchester 904-984 AD)

24.
Good God,
give ear to my words;
hearken to my voice,
my meditation and cry.
You are my governor,
to you I pray.
Like the psalmist,
I can feel
I am cast from your sight.
Yet,
you hear the voice
of my supplication
when I cry,
and you give grace
even before I plead. Amen.

Prayers I Pray for the Sick and the Dead

25.
Name our
fellow departed
today.
Pray
They are clothed
by Christ
from the beginning
of creation.
White robed
Name each one.
Pray upon them
The benefit of
Christ's enrobing
of our nature,
restoring of it,
uniting all creation
and creatures
with God,
and us one to another,
eternally
conjoined
in divine communion. Amen.

26.
Ring for joy,
ring for pain,
ring for love,
ring for
our risen dead.
Ring for
the blessed births,
ring for
the sin-sick soul,
ring
and beckon the lost!
Ring,
O blessed bells,
that we may serve,
kneel,
and stand
united in prayer
for parents,
brothers, sisters,
siblings, and friends.
Ring bells for the dead
And for the living dead. Amen.

27.
I give thanks
for those I love but see no longer,
and for those
I still have to love
and hold.
In loving,
we are inextricably joined
with those who have gone before.
So
Set out the meal,
join the parade,
play cards,
laugh,
and tell stories,
for they are with me.
in this way,
I imagine eternity breaks in. Amen.

28.
God,
I have
such a capacity
for self-delusion
I hold
my personal
vision of you constricted.
Help me then
set my self idea
aside
Help me
Set unlock
My asphyxiated
Vision of you
to see
how the life
of Jesus
changes
how I see
the God of all,
the world
God has made,
the people
of his making. Amen.

(Inspired by Rowan Williams)

29.
Dear God,
A bit of prayer,
grant me so to love you
that I come to know you.
Grant me so to seek
to know you
that I come to love you. Amen

30.
Good lord
who has created
my body to feel
and touch,
my eyes
and ears,
my body
to experience
your creation,
help
my fundamental being
to be enlivened
by the
ecstatic experience
of its revelation.
I bid your wisdom
speak as

31.
I fumble
towards the
Heavenly Father.
I am always reaching out
beyond myself,
so direct my body,
my mind,
my spirit
away from my
incompleteness
to you. Amen.

Inspired by the work of theologian Erich Przywara.)

32.
Today,
I walked beneath
the hanging names
of lynched Black citizens.
I touched those
from Texas.
God you weep
for your hung children,
Lord.
May
I be reckoned
by your cross
to the horror
of the past,
whispering a vision
anew from
death to life,
where all stand
without fear,
justice held
arm in arm
against evil. Amen.

33.
Dear wild God,
come to my table,
break my porcelain,
bend my fork,
eat all my mustard,
and tarnish my silver.
Make wine from my vinegar.
I fear you,
for you remind me
of something dark
I have dreamt,
and the secrets
I wish you didn't know.
Smoke your pipe
and dance a jig
with my black dog.
Then raise my head
to dance with you,
throw my peas,
and heal the dog,
and let go of my
broken memories. Amen.

34.
I watched
the old woman sweep,
again,
then wet the cobblestone
from her tin bucket
to wet the dust
and shine the rock.
Old woman God
discover
my cobblestoned heart;
sweep out the dregs
that lay there
that accumulate there.
Wash me through with blessed water
that my heart may crack,
and
shine with
life and light. Amen.

35.
God of darkness,
God of light,
help me to know your presence
when night comes,
and fear whispers to me.
When the stories of death
and ghosts haunt me,
help me remember
that you are the end
as you are the beginning,
and that such monsters
do not have the last word. Amen.

36.
God of darkness,
God of light,
help me to know your presence
when night comes,
and fear whispers to me.
When the stories of death
and ghosts haunt me,
help me remember
that you are the end
as you are the beginning,
and that such monsters
do not have the last word. Amen.

37.
Anxiety, fear,
and depression
are not sins.
The Bible suggests
that Jesus felt
sadness and anxiety.
To suggest Jesus
was neurotypical
is to suggest he was
less human
or non-feeling
than all humanity.
We are feeling creatures,
and Christ joined us
in embodiment
with all those feelings. Amen.

38.
A friend reminded me
it's easy to have hope
when things are good.
It takes courage
to have hope
when things are tough.
Patient and good Lord,
give me courage to hope
in things unseen
and face my trials,
faith to remember
you are with me,
in love
and walk
with me eternally. Amen.

39.
Let me step humbly with you
Upon the cross
And into death's tomb
Then to lie in wait
Like a secret watcher
as you conquer sin
and trample death.
Then let me bow
my meek head
as I share in my undeserved
unasked for
but desperately needed
deliverance. Amen.

40.
God labors on
with me,
Jesus's strife
remains
as a potter
and founder
in his foundry
to encourage
in me a death
such as his
for the world.
Mold me,
fire me,
that
I may
preach a lively word
and encourage
humanity's
ministry to humanity. Amen.

41.
The mystery of the Eucharist
is a web of bodily
and spiritual experiences
woven into our cosmos,
part of experiencing heaven
and the other side
of the eschaton.
Help us not to consume
for our own needs alone,
but to live our lives with others,
so that they too
are woven into God's embrace.
The heavenly banquet
set before us
is unified in
mystical communion
with God
through the mystery
of Christ and the Spirit.
These are epiphany like events,
part of a heaven
yet to come
for the body-bound.
Its purpose in this world
is for the living of life
and the goodness of all. Amen.

42.
Wasteful,
wild Lord,
you recklessly
sow the Gospel seeds,
you leaven
all the flour at once,
you turn the house
upside down
for the lost,
and you do not
count the cost
of opening the gate
of your kingdom.
Let me
be so generous
with all,
and especially with myself. Amen.

43.
Garden God,
God of Sinai,
and God of the
peak of the Temple Mount,
seek after
us in our hiding,
 shepherd us in
our wandering,
and be our might,
freeing us from
worldly desires
for power.
Teach us to
depend upon you,
proclaim your name,
and do your good. Amen

44.
Risen Lord,
give us the courage
to overcome
our fear
and speak the
Good News of salvation
like Mary, Joanna, and Magdalene.
Help us to
offer our bodies
as your crucified hands
and feet,
to go
and act out salvation,
and speak an encouraging word
of your saving grace. Amen.

45.
The darkest
things are the hungriest,
and they are attracted
to the beautiful
and the good.
Keep me safe
in the night
from all my hauntings.
Deliver me
from the wakefulness
of worries and preoccupations,
and let me rest,
for your burden is light,
and your yoke is easy.
Come and let
Me rest in thee. Amen.

46.
The days are so dark now.
Come, O come, Light of God.
Bring warmth
to where to my heart
that is cold,
tenderness to where
mine is stone,
mercy to where I am broken,
love when I have nothing more to give,
and believe I have lost it
and can't remember where or when. Amen.

47.

I

Walk the pilgrim journey,
step by step,
day by day,
prayer by prayer,
a bodily experience of mortality
and also of hope in Christ.
The poet whispers eternal words,
I listen.
The bridegroom gestures,
I look.
The ancient mariner's eye holds me,
I don't move, then,
A step towards the door,
the banquet awaits. Amen.

Inspired by Samuel Taylor Coleridge's "The Rime of the Ancient Mariner," 1797

48.
Gracious God
help me
to preach the Gospel
lead where it may,
cost what it will.
Help me lay down
my the selfishness
in my soul.
Give me strength
that my will
may stand strong
against idolatry,
against temptation,
and lead me simply
to do
that which God
would have me to do,
easy or difficult.
That at the last day,
death
having been rent asunder,
my sins forgiven,
that I may stand
in your house
before your throne
and join the saints in light
praising you. Amen.

Prayers I Pray in the Day and at the Night

49.
Christ,
You are the morning star
awaken us.
When the night
of this world is past,
remember us.
Give to us muddlers,
sinners,
and the overcome,
the promise of the light of life.
For those
who dwell
in darkness
shall gaze upon
everlasting day. Amen.

50.
Joy comes
in the morning;
may we pause
and breathe it in.
Give thanks for the day,
for the gift of life,
for friends when trouble lurks,
and for the goodness we have.
Without such beginnings,
we will spend the day in scarcity and shadow. Amen.

51.
Help me be mindful of God.
Be mindful of one another.
Be mindful of the good.
Be mindful of my body.
Be mindful of Christ's body.
Be mindful. Amen.

52.
Evening comes,
day is done,
we reflect
and know
in our
deepest moments
we have said
the most
inadequate things.
So gladden
our hearts
because darkness
is forever
drawn to light,
but light is light
and does not know it
so the light absorbs
it by nature,
so our darkness
meets its
own extinguishment.
So let us
be like trees
whose roots
are deep
in the dark soil
and stretch
our limbs to the light,
let this be our character. Amen.

(Inspired by Edna O'Brien.)

53.
On this day
may I have
the faith of
Mary Magdalene
to share my faith
first
by giving thanks
and time to
worship and pray;
and then
may I have such faith
as to speak to
the hidden,
fearful,
and questioning
saying:
there is good news today! Amen.

54.
Do not repay
suffering with suffering.
Our suffering
has no meaning
but is redeemed
because Christ
suffers and rises.
Therefore,
our practice
is to repay
suffering
with meaning
and raise
what is dead
with love,
mercy,
and peace. Amen.

55.
Jesus
gives thanks
to God
for the people.
We are seen
as gifts to God,
no longer sacrificial means
but gifts.
It is
our true humanity
in Jesus
that helps us
see each other
as gifts too.
Dear God,
let me see
each person today
in my life
as a gift from God
and practice the art of
gratitude. Amen.

56.
Dear wakeful Lord,
watch over us as the sun
makes its way across our horizons.
Let us see anew the day before us.
While your narrative of love arcs across time,
we have moments to offer you.
So let us act with love in the opportunities before us. Amen.

57.
O God,
you have folded back
the mantle of night
and clothed us with
the golden glory
of the day.
Chase from our hearts
all gloomy thoughts
and make us glad
with the brightness of your hope,
that today we may aspire
to unwon virtue. Amen.

(Inspired by *With God in Prayer*, Charles Henry Brent, 1907)

58.
Gracious Creator,
I give thanks
not only for the
food
that sustains my
body today,
but for
the beauty
that nourishes
my soul.
So remind me
to say grace
before the play
and the opera.
For the stories
that reveal truth
and stir my heart.
Remind me
to say grace
before a concert,
For the hymns
And songs
that lift my spirit,
bring me joy,
and lead me
to you.
I want to
say grace
before I open a book,
For the words
that teach
and transform me.
Help me say grace
before sketching,
painting,
For the creativity
and movement
that mirror

Your own
boundless imagination.
I want to
say grace
before walking,
playing, fishing,
hiking, camping,
and dancing and singing
by the fire.
Remind me
To say grace
For the gift of strength,
rhythm,
and the delight
of simply being alive.
Hallelujah.
I say grace for my keypad and pen,
For the privilege of expressing
My thoughts, dreams, and prayers.
Lord,
may every act,
however small,
be a reflection
of my gratitude
for the gift of life. Amen.

(Inspired by G K Chesterton's words on gratitude.)

59.
To say that Christ makes us one,
that we are made
brothers, sisters, siblings,
sons and daughters
in God's family,
is to make a claim
of kinship.
This is rehearsed
in baptism
and invites us
to familial reciprocity
instead of competition.
Here the Christian prays to God
And says to each: "You are my kin, I love you." Amen.

60.
As I prepare for bed,
dearest Lord,
remember me
and mine,
As a drinker I drink
and as a swearer I swear,
I've been known
For singin' there,
and dancin' here
laughing and caring on
nevertheless
look upon us all with
mercies temporal and divine!
For the glory shall be thine! Amen!

(Inspired by Robert Burns's, *Holy Willie's Prayer*, 1785.)

Prayers I Pray for Creation

61.

Oh, wild God
whose fingers
bring forth the trees
and hair the brambles.
You give the dormice
and wood mice shelter.
The foxes
and badger
receive their dens.
The crow a perch
to see
and voles
earth to till.
In your embracing arms
woodpigeons coo
while
the flycatchers,
nuthatches,
finches,
and blackcaps nest.
In return
they glorify you
with their very existence
among
your brambled oak
and flowered down. Amen.

62.
Dear God,
of cosmos
and beyond
our knowing,
when we contemplate thee,
we are reminded
no king
or governor
can hold
thy fullest light
in our darkness.
You are maker
and friend filled
with light, life, and joy enough
if we but behold thee day by day.
You do not govern
nor rule from
the shadowed world
but instead
from eternal grace
shed from cross and tomb.
So wash us
good governor
that we might touch
heavenly places
in this life
and thus know
the promise of life to come.
Amen.

63.
Gracious God,
we give thanks
for your boundless love,
the gift of creation,
for family, friends,
and the mercy shown in Christ
the King of Kings.
Fill our hearts
with gratitude
that overflows
into lives of service. Amen.

64.
At morn,
robins praised
your name;
at midday,
the first spring
butterflies flashed
the emerald colors
of your grace;
at eve,
the armadillo
gave thanks for grubs,
and the coyote
hallowed
the beauty
of your moon
and the gift of family.
May we pause
to give glory
at the wonders
of your hand. Amen.

65.
You brought forth
creation
for you are a
wholly creative God
of active power
and might.
You are the God
Who created
the cosmos,
the world,
and all there in.
What a radical
Belief that
brings to mind
all kinds of creative possibilities
for humankind.
Do not let
Me wait your invitation
For such unrequited
possibilities
grow dim,
dark,
and wither.
Help me
not only imagine
and pray
to you
creative God
but to embrace
our work as co-creators,
reversing the earth's
lack of flourishing
and decline. Amen.

(Inspired by Athanasius' *First Letter to Serapion*)

66.
God
who has seen
all of the cosmos
and loves
Your creatures
through the
eyes of Christ,
help me see the world
with your eyes,
to listen to it
with your ears,
and to love
with your heart.
Amen.

Inspired by *Andrei Rublev*, Andrei Tarkovsky's film, 1966)

Prayers I Pray for Workers

67.
Early they rise,
I honor you.
Before the sun rises,
the night people
finish their last tasks:
deliver the clean laundry
and sheets,
produce for the market,
papers to doors,
fresh baked goods
for the hungry.
We do not see you normally,
but when we do,
we see angels
of the night
tending and caring.
Bless you, the night people. Amen.

68.
Pray for the worker,
the worker who:
digs, paves, mows, welds,
binds steel, climbs in attics,
and cleans the traps.
Sing the praise
of those who work
in factories,
and mines,
who give thanks
at their table
when family's about,
and wake up
to toil
night and day
by hand and by brain,
to earn their pay,
who for centuries past
worked
for no more
than their bread.
We all depend upon them,
our invisible workers
whom God glorifies,
alive and dead. Amen.

(Inspired by *The Worker's Song,* The Dropkick Murphy's, 2020)

69.
Bless hands and hearts,
give tenacity and perseverance,
to those who clean and wipe,
wash windows and dust,
who mop and sweep.
They are inconspicuous
and unseen to most.
Yet they are there
at the coffee shop,
diner, retail store,
and hotels.
God grants dignity,
for they are Christ's friends.
The God who washes feet
blesses their work and sees the unseen. Amen.

70.
Lord,
thank you
for those who work
and labor today:
those in the kitchen,
yes,
and those at the airport,
in taxis,
store clerks,
fast-food servers,
the police,
firefighters,
doctors,
and nurses.
As we give thanks,
we remember you,
your friends,
and their families too. Amen.

71.
God of darkness,
God of light,
help me to know your presence
when night comes,
and fear whispers to me.
When the stories of death
and ghosts haunt me,
help me remember
that you are the end
as you are the beginning,
and that such monsters
do not have the last word. Amen.

72.
Praise the Cooks,
restaurant, and bar workers
who work into the wee hours.
Lord, bless the hands
that wash the last glass,
who mop the last corner,
steam the last dish,
and count the food
for tomorrow's orders.
Hallow the all-nighters
who keep the coffee fresh,
orders fast,
and bus and wipe off our tables.
Help us notice the unnoticed. Amen.

73.
Pentecost for the laborer:
Lord God of flame,
so burn in our hearts
that when we,
as the Church,
speak and act,
the laborer may hear
in our words
and see in our actions
the Gospel tongues
announcing
the suffering servant's freedom message.
Save the suffering,
soothe the aches,
fill the larder with good food. Amen.

74.
End my day
By bringing to mind,
God who remembers
Your own,
one person
who crossed my path:
a gas station attendant,
a food worker,
a grocery clerk,
a person who cleans.
Remind me first to give thanks for them,
thank them for their work,
their friends and families,
and pray for their going and coming.
For they are your greatest treasure
Remind me too,
to be a person who might
Be remembered for service and servanthood. Amen.

75.
Bless the shopkeeper;
she takes care
of her family,
cleans up,
and makes her way.
Lunch packed,
she opens the door,
sets out her wares,
and sits and waits.
She looks for the shopper
who appreciates
what she offers.
After conversation
and a sale,
she puts her hand out,
small and wrinkled,
and says,
"Thank you.
It was nice to meet you."
I say the same because it is true.
Bless the shopkeeper. Amen.

76.
Consider this:
Christ-like work
is Martha work,
for it is servant work.
Christ prepares
a room for us,
sets the table for us,
and washes away our sins.
Help me become
a follower who acts
to welcome all,
make a place
at the table for all,
and forgive the sins of all. Amen.

77.
Watch over,
Lord,
the byway's
and the
workers
of the road.
In ice and snow,
they warm their cabins,
turn on their lights,
and go out to scrape,
plow,
and salt
the roads
for our safety.
As we make our way,
raise to heaven
our gratitude
for all
who make
our days easier,
even those
we never see
or know. Amen.

78.
For the cracked hands
of the farmers
and the backs
of migrant field workers,
for the aches and pains
of the ranchers,
for their early hours
and hard work,
for the health
and fruitfulness
of their sowing,
and good care
of their livestock,
Amen.

79.
Dear generous God,
Who made sabbath
For humanity,
We thank you for
tea and biscuits.
Whether
we work
in construction
or drive big lorries,
We thank you for
tea and biscuits.
If we clean houses
or work as cooks
or washing dishes all day,
We thank you for
tea and biscuits.
If we work
in schools
or universities,
work the trains,
open doors,
wash clothes,
or drive a car for a living,
We thank you for
tea and biscuits.
For surely as it must be in heaven,
So make it so on earth
give us today
our daily tea and biscuit. Amen.

(For my American friends: biscuits are cookies, and lorries are trucks.
Inspired by Billy Connolly, *Windswept and Interesting*, 2021.)

Prayers I Pray for the Artist and Beauty
80.
Pray for the poets.
Let the words
come out
of your soul
like a rocket.
Write to us
with the words
of the first people.
Do not hide
from us
what you see,
experience,
love,
and lose.
Write to us
of everyday
life
where God moves;
do not leave out the sorrows,
desires,
and passing thoughts.
Remind us of beauty,
dreams,
and riches
found in the
poverty of places
to which
we are indifferent.
Sing to the Creator God,
and let us listen.

(Inspired by Rainer Maria Rilke's letter to young poet Franz Xaver
Kappus)

81.
God of beauty-making,
what manner of things
you have made!
We give thanks
for the artists who paint,
photograph,
throw clay,
work with hypermedia,
and sculpt.
In their work,
we see glimpses
of the cosmic
beauty distilled in Christ,
through whom all things are made. Amen.

82.
May we always
have beautiful experiences
of the mysterious.
Wonder as a fundamental emotion,
standing at the cradle
of true art and science.
May we always wonder and marvel.
For if we lack curiosity,
our eyes dimmed,
we cannot comprehend you
O God.

(Inspired by Albert Einstein)

Prayers I Pray for the World We I Live In

83.
God of the cosmos,
healer of the breach,
lover of the poor,
the ill,
and orphaned,
give us wisdom
in electing officials
for our country.
Help us
become a people
of peace-making,
a blessing and servant
to the least among our citizens,
and eager
to assist other nations
of your earth. Amen.

84.
Governor of the cosmos,
watch over
our engagement
in the dual citizenship
of your reign
and this earthly nation.
Help us choose
wisely those
who will govern
 for the good
and just use
of our resources.
Remind us that our
freedom comes
with responsibility
to you and to others. Amen.

85.
Every generation
has its holy innocents,
created by the powers
and principalities of this world.
God of love and shelter,
unfold your wing
of mercy over all innocent victims.
Frustrate the political designs of evil.
Help us take part
in establishing your rule of justice,
love, and peace. Amen
God of the Abrahamic faiths
Of Judaism,
Islam,
and Christianity,
we pray
for peace
in Jerusalem.
May those
who love you
and live together
prosper
and work together
for peace
within your walls.
Let peace
come to our
friends and relatives
wherever they may be.
For your sake,
let us seek your peace
beyond understanding. Amen.

86.
You are a lily in the field,
a bird of the air,
a sheep in search of green pastures,
and a hart thirsty for living water
more: you are you.
Wherever you are,
whoever you are,
you are loved by God
for the very existence of you
and embraced as kin
by God's kiss of grace. Amen.

87.
Loving Lord,
help us grasp
the faithful work
of loving someone
who is against us
because
they think
differently.
Teach us
that shutting
off the discourse,
giving up,
or going our own way
because of what
others might think,
is not loving,
but heartless.
By setting aside
the objects
of the present life
that fill
the human eye
with false magnification
due to immediacy,
grant us
patience
to take
the long view.
Help us understand
that listening
and building cruciform relationships,
based upon your example,
is the only Christian way. Amen.
(Inspired by William Wilberforce)

Prayers I Pray For Jesus' Birth

88.
Dear Lord,
the New Year passes,
yet not all has ended.
Many things continue
some haunt us,
some we work on,
some are physical
or cancerous.
As the web of our lives continues
death and renewal
give us grace
that old times be forgotten
while you strengthen
friendships held dear. Amen.

89.
Satan's pow'r creates unrest.
Lord, give rest to your gentle people,
lift up our faces from dismay,
open our ears to good news of comfort.
Give us joy for our scorn,
courage for our fright.
Through angelic work,
may we brightly comfort
and bring joy to others.

90.
Angels and Archangels
travel with me,
Cherubim and Seraphim,
let us take flight together.
May we join with Mary
and worship
our beloved
with a kiss.
Then help me
in the bleak midwinter
and in the morning of life
to give Christ my heart. Amen.

(Inspired by Christina Rossetti's *In The Bleak Midwinter*, 1872.)

91.
Walk down the road
at set of sun
to Bethlehem,
pause and listen near the manger
for Mary singing to her child among the hay.
Then consider the least,
the lost, the poor,
and the hungry who long
for this son's love song.
May we sing it still. Amen.

(Inspired by Margaret Rose's *The Little Road to Bethlehem*, 1946.)

92.
Ring a bell for
Christmas Day,
sing a carol or two,
say "Peace to you,
dear friend."
For while hate is strong
and mocks the day,
it shall not win,
but be turned upside down
by the God who loves
and makes us kin.
So make merry
before its bowed head
for victory comes in the manger bed. Amen.

93.
Open our eyes,
O Holy Night.
Brightly shine stars,
as if the day of your birth!
Let our souls feel
a thrill of hope
at God's wondrous love.
Weary world, rejoice!
Night divine—hear angels' voices
break our chains
and shepherd in the Prince of Peace. Amen.

94.
Wake,
awake,
let our night fly,
hear the watch crying!
Listen,
for darkness hears welcome
angel's voices.
Light our lamps;
tomorrow we rehearse
the marriage between
heaven and earth,
for what was made
of earthenware
is now remade for eternity. Amen.

95.
Let heralds cry,
"Comfort, comfort my people!"
Tell of peace,
lighten the mourning
of sorrow's load.
Say to the valley,
"Rise up!"
Tell the hill, "Bow down,"
so the weak need
not suffer to meet the Savior.
Come,
thou-universal blessing,
show us perfect peace
and joy unceasing.
Remove from hearts
devilish pride
and brutal passions.
Let all the beloved
sinners saved pant
for greater presence till,
anew created,
we behold your glorious
natal image retrieved. Amen.

(Inspired by Charles Wesley's hymn *And Can It Be That I Should Gain?*, 1738 .)

96.
Let us awake,
the night dies before us.
Let dawn banish sadness,
the rising sun bring gladness.
Arise to greet
the Prince of Morning;
let us join him
and bring peace,
love, and mercy.

(HT Melvin Lloyd Farrell)

97.
Come tomorrow
our dancing day;
and call us,
True Love,
to your dance.
Come and be born
among us,
take our flesh
and substance,
knit us to the divine.
From the manger,
enwrap us all,
that in love
we may dance together.

(Inspired by a Cornish Carol, *Tomorrow Shall Be My Dancing Day*)

98.
We hope and hope
help us hope
for a deeper connection to you.
For God of all being,
you are my longing
through and through,
so Dayspring from on high,
be near,
and Daystar
in my heart appear.
Let me not wait in hope
without design,
but awaken me to your closeness.

(Inspired by Charles Wesley, "Christ, Whose Glory Fills the Skies," 1738.)

Prayers I Pray for A Holy Week Before Easter

99.
You come
beneath your station,
and sit us at the table,
offering again
a vision of your sacrifice.
We betray our faith
by shrinking from the cross.
We sleep
when asked to wake,
seek violence
when invited to peace,
and fall silent
when asked to speak.
Let your cross awake us,
grant peace. Amen.

100.
Grant me to walk with you,
the road where palms
and
scattered garments
now decay.
Let angels
look upon me
and see
my approaching
to your sacrifice. Amen.

101.
We repent
for the sons and daughters
whom we bore to you,
whom we sacrificed
and let be devoured.
We slaughtered your children
and delivered them
up as offerings
by fire to our
demons of personal freedom
instead of responsibility.
We defile ourselves
with all our idols. Amen.
Preach
this passion
tide
so our wasted bones
may rattle,
that we might be bound
again with sinew,
flesh, and skin.
And, when we call
"See, our hope is lost!"
Remind us
of God's promise
to open our graves,
end death's rule,
and bring us up.
Breathe out upon us
Preacher
Of the good news
of Christ's cross,
see us rise up,
thy slain and walking dead.
Sleepers awake! Amen.

102.
We are your creatures,
O God,
parted by the gulf of sin.
Bring us back!
Recover us
as your own.
Release us
from what binds us
by the work
of your cross.
Trample the devil
under your feet,
and keep death
in its grave.
Love us
who had s
ought another god
instead of you. Amen.

(Inspired by Origen)

103.
Your acts reveals
your nature so
Unblind our eyes,
unstop our ears,
as creation breaks
a silence before the cross
God's monument of victory
to all bodies
the broken,
dispossessed,
and enslaved.
Sun,
veil your face;
earth,
quake;
mountain,
rend asunder.
That I may participate
as your beloved creature. Amen.

(Inspired by Athanasius.)

A Prayers I Pray You My Dear Reader, Saint and Sinner

104.
Sinners
become saints
through
quiet lives,
faithful,
crazed acts,
wild belief,
and silent solitude.
From wilderness
to town,
monastery
and hermitage,
with the poorest
of the poor,
sick,
and dying,
the saints
are the very best
of whom
you and I might become.
God bless the
You sinner
and saint
of our devotion.
You and I
live and love,
knit into this
mystical body
imagined
in the mind of God
and made flesh.
Bless us
You and me
with
the wisdom of communion
so as to envision

the ineffable joys
of eternity prepared
from the first breath
of the cosmos. Amen.

(Inspired by the Episcopal service for All Hallows' Eve)

Acknowledgments

I want to thank JoAnne, my wife, who is always my first reader. Her red pen takes care of the commas and poor grammar. Marcea Paul also read it for heresy! She is a gifted pastor and teacher and contributed a good reflection on this text, for which I am grateful. Of course, I want to thank my staff, who have helped schedule and arrange my ministry so that I have time for prayer daily and protect my days off for prayer, writing, and time with family. In large part, this book is a fruition of their gift. Finally, I want to thank all of my readers who have said, "amen" to these prayers. I am grateful for your support and for our prayer together. You have encouraged me and I am grateful.

About the Author

C. Andrew Doyle has been the ninth Bishop of Texas for over a decade. During that time the Diocese of Texas has grown and he now oversees and pastors more than 78,000 parishioners and 400 clergy working in 177 congregations, 50 missional communities, 27 campus missions, 57 schools, and 10 institutions. Bishop Doyle received his M.Div. from Virginia Theological Seminary after receiving a fine arts degree from the University of North Texas. Previous to his election in 2008, Bishop Doyle served for five years as Canon to the Ordinary. He also served churches in Temple and College Station, as well as being elected deputy to several General Conventions. He most recently served on the Structure Committee and is currently president of the Compass Rose Society, a global group of patrons and leaders making a difference in the Anglican Communion. He has led the creation of two new foundations. He is known for his creative and strategic thinking, his advocacy for the immigrant and migrant, his work in stewardship and development, and most recently for the creation of a Racial Justice initiative with a 13 million dollar corpus.

He describes his six-word autobiography as: "Met Jesus on pilgrimage, still walking." Bishop Doyle's focus for ministry is challenging Episcopalians to move into their communities with the Gospel in word and action. He is a preacher, a teacher, and a speaker. He has been interviewed on CBS, in *Newsweek*, *Texas Monthly*, and for *Wired*. His teaching mixes references from pop culture's music and movies with the latest in secular leadership trends in order to reach the broadest spectrum of readers.

His books include: *Unabashedly Episcopalian: The Good News of the Episcopal Church*, 2012; *Orgullosamente Episcopal*, 2015; *Church: A Generous Community Amplified for the Future*, 2015; *A Generous Community: Being Church In A New Missionary Age*, 2015; *Small Batch: Local, Organic, and Sustainable Church*, 2016; *The Jesus Heist*, 2017; *Vocātiō: Imaging a Visible Church*, 2018; *Citizen: Faithful Discipleship in a Partisan World*, 2020; *Embodied Liturgy*, 2021; edited *Episcopate*, 2023; *Wrestling with Angels and Demons*, 2024; and *Unabashed Faith*, 2025.

Bishop Doyle is married to JoAnne Doyle and they have two daughters. He is a vinyl collector, reader, artist, banjo player, and fly fisherman.

Prayer Journal

The following pages are provided so that you may write down your favorite prayers, your thoughts that come from prayer, and notes from the prayers above. It is also so that you may write your own prayers. I hope you will. The prayers that are your own mixed with the prayers of others and found in books like The Book of Common Prayer 1979, can make for a deep prayer life in which God is speaking while you wrestle with angels and demons.

[Insert twenty pages with Prayer Journal at the top, so people can write prayers they love, or their own prayers and notes]

www.ingramcontent.com/pod-product-compliance
Lightning Source LLC
Chambersburg PA
CBHW071224090426
42736CB00014B/2967

9 781966 865612